101 THINGS

I WANT TO SAY...

THE COLLECTION

A Father's Advice to His Children
on Reaching a Passage in Their Lives

**To My Daughter, Meghan,
on Beginning College**

**To My Son, Joshua,
on Graduating College**

**To My Daughter, Andrea,
on Beginning Her Career**

Douglas J. Wood

ISBN: 1499727453
ISBN-13: 9781499727456

Author's Note

I have three wonderful children, all of whom are now young adults and on their own—Meghan is a prosecutor in Miami, Joshua is an entrepreneur who owns an advertising agency in New York City, a brewery, and is developing a real estate project in Allentown, Pennsylvania, and Andrea is a physical therapist in Boston.

When each of them reached a significant passage in their lives, I shared the advice that follows. I hope you find it enjoyable, at times humorous, at times serious, but at all times heartfelt. They are printed in the order I wrote them. I think readers will see that as they matured, so did I.

Whatever success my children have achieved, however, is very much credited to Carol Ann, my wife and partner of more than 40 years. This book is dedicated to her.

To My Daughter, Meghan, on Beginning College

1

Boys are pigs.

2

Listen to your heart. You're good at that, and it's a part of you that I truly admire. It's what makes you such a special person in so many ways.

3

Listen to your head. While you're pretty good at that, too, as your father, I can't tell you often enough to use your head. Perhaps a rule of thumb ought to be to listen first with your heart, then with your head, and then go with the heart as long as your head doesn't tell you to think twice.

4

Even those who are innocent are often found guilty. Guilty by association is one of the cruelest things we ever face. It takes on many forms. So watch out where you are, whom you're with, and what others around you are doing. Wrong place, wrong time is all too often a harsh lesson in life.

5

Unfortunately, life has a calendar. Don't let things pass you by. The timid lead timid lives. The intrepid lead exciting lives. And while that doesn't mean you should be stupid in what you do, you should certainly take on challenges as opportunities, not threats.

6

Boys are pigs.
Oh yeah, I already mentioned that.

7

There's always a worse alternative. But that doesn't mean the alternative presented is necessarily a good one. Don't automatically settle for what's offered. If the alternative presented is unacceptable, reject it. Never accept the lowest common denominator because something else would be worse. Be patient. Wait for the right alternative, not necessarily what's offered.

8

Procrastination limits one's possibilities. The easiest thing to be is lazy; the hardest thing to be is ahead of the curve—out front. Don't confuse the need to relax, sleep, hide, run, or whatever method of avoidance suits the moment with putting off what needs to be done. You'll know when you're procrastinating. No one will have to tell you. Only you can be fooled by your own excuses. You're better than that.

9

Just being there has benefits. Don't skip classes. Simply by sitting in class, you learn a lot more than you do reading stuff back at the dorm or in the library. It may even mean the difference of a full letter grade.

10

College is a time for you to be educated, not bored. On many occasions, high school was boring. Lectures. Memorization. College, on the other hand, is truly a time for you to learn, to be challenged, and to overcome challenges presented to you. If you accept anything in college as just another boring class, boring teacher, or boring subject, you lose sight of the most important four years in your lifetime. That's true of even the mandatory courses. To paraphrase Dorothy from *The Wizard of Oz*, "You're not in Wyckoff anymore."

11

Boys have a lot in common with pigs. Gettin' the idea?

12

Sooner or later, it's hard for everyone. Everyone in college faces tough courses, difficult professors, and unfair days. Over time, you either succumb to the disappointments or overcome the obstacles. That's your choice. Learn from the hard lessons.

13

Call home. Often.

14

E-mail me. Often.

15

There's nothing you don't want to tell me that I don't want to hear. Well, OK, I do suppose there are some things I really don't *need* to hear. But I'd rather be told than surprised.

16

Let me know if you'd like to take a break on a weekend and come home. You may even find that you occasionally get homesick. You might actually miss a home-cooked meal and your own bed. It's all there whenever you want it, even if the bed might have been moved into another room. While in the future a lot of your time at home will be for visits, you'll never be a visitor.

17

Let others help. In fact, ask for it. Remember how you learned in your freshman year of high school that you really didn't need to be nervous once some upperclassmen helped you understand the system? College can be even more intimidating. But unlike in high school, everyone in college is there for a focused reason, and the faculty is there to help you. Get to know your professors. Get to know the administration. You saw how that worked for you in high school. It will work even more in college.

18

Some pigs are nice pigs, but most pigs aren't. I know what you're thinking: *Daddy, I know what to do.* Famous last words. Don't let any boy, ever, treat you with disrespect, bully you, demean you, or so much as touch you without your permission.

19

Don't worry about getting me my money's worth from your college education. College is your deal. Make the money I invest work for you, not me.

20

Help others. That comes naturally to you, so enough said.

21

Watch what upperclassmen do. Divide them into two categories—the movers and shakers, and the idiots. Try to follow the former and keep the occasions on which you follow the latter to a minimum. But even if you should happen to act like one of the idiots, don't get too down on yourself. Just don't do it twice.

22

Pigs. Boys. Redundant.

23

Remember your faith. While it's not all-important that you go to a church or that you have anything to do with organized religion, it is important that you keep your faith in God. Understand that there are things far greater than any of us that put you on this earth for more than the purpose of waking up in the morning and going to sleep at night. Keep your faith by knowing that every day you've done what's right in your heart and in your head. And when you stumble in your faith, pull yourself up, do better, and don't repeat the mistake.

24

Caller ID is the evil twin of call waiting. The former is an excuse to hide from others you know; the latter is a reason not to miss hearing from those who care.

25

When I call you, return my call.
Quickly.

26

When I e-mail you, e-mail me back.
Quickly.

27

Blood is thicker than friendship, and the two together are more powerful than either alone. Never forget family and what it's meant to you in the last eighteen years. Never forget all the friendships you've nourished in those years—remember the friendship that your siblings offer you as well. Keep in touch with everyone. Call them, e-mail them, and see them when you can. But remember first and foremost that your family is what got you to where you are. Regardless of how crazy they can sometimes make you feel, never reject them or leave them behind, and always remember that they are your friends, too.

28

There are plenty of pigs to choose from. Choose wisely. Don't choose too early. See what the farm has to offer. I think you'll find that the vast majority rightfully goes off to slaughter. Make sure you get the pick of the litter.

29

Leading is always better than following. You've always been a leader. Of the many things that make me so proud of you, your ability to lead others by example and decisive action is among the most impressive. Throughout your high-school years, when someone needed to be helped, needed to be remembered, or needed to be reminded, you took it upon yourself to lead the charge. Don't lose that in the college environment of thousands of students and acres of campus. On day one, all freshmen are the same. There's no reason you can't step out in front. Just watch your back occasionally, but never fear a road ahead where you're looking down new, rather than worn-out, paths.

30

Try to give back more than you take. As you get older, days go faster and regrets come sooner unless you remember, every day, to give back a little to those who give to you. I have no doubt that such an approach to life comes easily for you. You are a natural nurturer of others and one who gives back intuitively. Regardless, always ask yourself every day if you've given back a little here and there so that in the end, you've taken less than you've given. You've got a lifetime ahead of you to do so, but every day counts.

31

"Oink, oink, grunt, grunt." "Want to go to a movie?" Don't confuse the two.

32

Say you're sorry when you've done something wrong. Mean it when you say it. "Sorry" is all too common an excuse rather than a true regret. More importantly, when people say that they're "sorry," they're asking for forgiveness that they do not deserve unless their regret is truthful. But if you believe in what you say, never apologize for it. Defend it, even if it angers someone. On occasion, you've done that with me. You've stuck to your guns. And on many of those occasions, I've come to realize you were right. And where I believed you were wrong, that's irrelevant, as long as any failure to apologize was because of your beliefs and not your pride.

33

When you are wrong, don't wait for people to ask you to say you're sorry, even if those people never say they're sorry to you when they're wrong. And when people truthfully say they're sorry for something they've done to you, accept the apology with grace. It's up to you whether you want to forgive them for what they've done.

34

Pick up what you put down. You know what I'm talking about. A mess in a place that's your own is one thing. A mess in someplace you share is quite another. And the quid pro quo applies as well— others should pick up whatever they've put down, too. Don't let them get away with anything less.

35

I won't bore you with the drugs, alcohol, and tobacco lecture. Been there, done that. I firmly believe you're far too intelligent to fall prey to drugs or tobacco, and that you will keep your alcohol consumption at a manageable level. At this point in your life, however, please remember that peer pressure will take on new meaning and that you will see stupid behavior displayed far more openly than you've ever seen it before. Don't get sucked into stupidity by association. You're too smart for that.

36

If you don't like what someone else does—particularly your roommate—follow the "twenty-four-hour rule." Don't be judgmental too quickly. Let twenty-four hours pass. And if the issue is still bothering you after a day, then bring it up. Voice your concern. Just remember that being too quick with a complaint can often make little annoyances insurmountable problems.

37

There's no longer anyone to nag you except you. No one will be calling you in the morning to get you up. No one will be bitching at you to clean your room, wash your clothes, do your homework, take a shower, eat a meal, or do an errand. That's all up to you now. You have to keep on top of yourself. Nag yourself. After all, if you don't do it, who will?

38

Petty, ignorant guys (PIGs) = barbarian, obnoxious yo-yos (BOYs).

39

For the most part, whatever has been done can be undone, even when it seems impossible to do so. All too often, when people regret something they've done or the way someone else has acted, they resign themselves to letting it ride. They believe that "what's done is done." Nothing could be further from the truth. With far less effort than one imagines, things can be changed. While that sometimes requires a little swallowing of pride and a broadened attitude, when it's important, it's all possible. Don't accept outcomes you later realize are mistakes simply because the effort needed to reverse them is difficult or, on first impression, even impossible.

40

As you've grown up in our family, you've broken the record for broken bones. But no broken bone has ever broken your spirit. That's good. Don't forget that being careful is a lot more intelligent than flirting with the odds. So please watch where you walk, stroll, amble, step, march, jump, hop, leap, climb, ascend, descend, ski, skate, or snowboard. You don't need the orthopedic wing of the local hospital named after you.

41

Party hearty, but party hardly. Don't overdo the party thing. College is notorious for parties, and deservedly so. Try to keep some sense of control and balance. It may sound like an old yarn, but academics first, party second. Confuse it too much, and you'll lose the former and never be able to again afford the latter.

42

Few things are done for you. Most things are done by you. Don't wait around for someone else to do what needs to be done. Chances are, no one will do it. If there's something you want accomplished, first determine to do it yourself. It that's not possible, next determine how you can do it with the help of someone else. And if that's not possible, find someone else who can do it, alone or together with others. If you follow that course of conduct, you'll likely never go beyond the second step in getting things done.

43

Step back from setbacks. Not everything you'll try to accomplish in college will be successful any more than it was when you were in high school. Just because you're older doesn't mean things are easier to realize. If you suffer a setback, step back. Take an objective look at the situation. Not much effort will reveal what you did wrong (if anything) or what obstacles you need to overcome to accomplish a task or achieve a goal on a second try. Your analysis may even resolve that it's not worth a second (or third or fourth or fifth) try.

44

Make sure you have the key to the gate, and don't let the local swine visit your pen without permission. It's that pig-boy thing again. So while your room might occasionally look like a pigsty, that doesn't mean you have to allow pigs in.

45

I've heard worse than anything you think is the worst. No matter what happens while you're in college (or for the rest of your life, for that matter), my role as your father is to provide you with support and comfort. But now that you're off to college, my ability to protect you is far more difficult. I can only hope you've learned enough in the past eighteen years to know better when faced with decisions between what's right and wrong or when you're in harm's way. Not necessarily because I taught you anything, but more likely because you taught it to yourself. All that matters is that you remember that I'm here. All you have to do is call.

46

Don't confuse school spirit with too many spirits. OK, OK—I said I wouldn't talk too much about the alcohol thing. Sorry. Just remember, while girls will be girls, boys will also be boys. And the more a girl's guard is down, the more the boy's... Hell, you get the idea.

47

Shortcuts in college are detours to disaster. You'll soon find that virtually every course has a shortcut created by upperclassmen or cheat-sheet publishers. And some of the shortcuts might even be pretty good. But they're options that are not worth the (lack of) effort. You're in college to learn, not to find a way to avoid what needs to be read, heard, written, recited, or most importantly, understood. Embrace why you're there, not how to take the easy way through the next four years.

48

Experiment with your brain, not your body. Yeah, yeah, yeah. It's the drugs-and-alcohol thing again. The point is that opportunities to stimulate your mind, as opposedtoyourbody,arealmostlimitless at a university like yours. Events. Special lectures. Concerts. Plays. Organizations. Government. Convocations. All sorts of things. There's never a reason to be bored. So learn your guitar, run for office, explore university life. Use, don't abuse, your brain.

49

Please refer to observation number one.
Thank you.

50

Keep a diary. Not just of what you did on a given day but more of what you thought about on a given day. Write it all down. Read what you've written. But keep it to yourself as a record of your personal thoughts. Share it with others sparingly, and only when you're convinced you've really thought it through. If you can somehow discipline yourself to keep such a diary, it will someday become the most important thing you've ever written.

51

Rule 1 on dancing: just because you step on your partner's foot, that's no reason not to dance. Rule 2 on dancing: regardless of how stupid you look dancing, someone else looks even worse. These rules also apply to life.

52

Your appetite to win should never be satisfied. Never go on a diet from victory. But don't be greedy about it either. Share your wins. Acknowledge those who helped you get there, because no one wins anything completely on his or her own. Never forget that.

53

If there's anything you can count on, you can count on your blessings—every day. So whenever you're in the dumps, just count your blessings.

54

Pessimism always breeds failure.

55

Optimism always breeds success. Pessimism doesn't even deserve to be on the same page.

56

Your first belief should be in yourself. Then in God. Then in others. Keep it in that order, and you'll do just fine.

57

While every job you do won't be excellent, you'll never achieve excellence if you set any less of a goal for yourself. When you do not achieve excellence, so be it. Forget it. Move on. But the more you make excellence your goal, the less the results will disappoint you.

58

People who don't have the courage to take risks risk what it's all about. Take risks, but don't be stupid. And when you fail, keep in mind what John Hersey, a famous author, once wrote: "Learning starts with failure; the first failure is the beginning of education."

59

Mind your mentors. Over time, you'll find people—professors, advisors, and elders—whom you particularly respect for their abilities and accomplishments. Get to know these people. Don't be shy. Learn how they learned to achieve. These people will become your mentors, from whom you'll learn a lot more than any book, lecture, or course will ever teach you.

60

Bureaucracy, bureaucrats, aristocracy, and autocrats are never to be trusted. Don't ever let them rule you. Be suspicious of authority.

61

Music does more than soothe the soul. It opens the mind and relaxes the body. You cannot listen to too much music.

62

Television soothes nothing. It's a form of escape. It closes your mind. And while there's nothing wrong with escaping, you can watch too much television. And computer games are even worse. Playing one is playing too many.

63

Don't believe in rules for the sake of having rules. Believe in rules when rules make sense. But before you reject a rule, think of who made it, why they made it, what it protects, and how you'd create a better rule to accomplish the right goal. If you can't do better, accept what others have ruled.

64

Respect your elders, the police, the unknown, and warning labels. If you do that, you'll be just fine.

65

Don't respect pigs.

66

Volunteer for volunteering's sake.

67

Be charitable without need for recognition. Those who give anonymously are truly charitable.

68

Help before you're asked.

69

If you mix the colors with the whites, it won't be the end of the world. And when in doubt, don't use bleach.

70

Never, ever, no matter what, under any circumstances, regardless of what may happen, lose your sense of humor.

71

Always be tolerant of others, but only if they are tolerant of you.

72

You do have physical limits. Respect them.

73

You don't have intellectual limits. Don't respect anyone who tells you otherwise.

74

A remote control really isn't all that important, so let the other person have it.

75

Boys. Maybe. Pigs. No.

76

Never drink anything you don't open yourself. And make sure it's never been opened before it's handed to you.

77

Coffee works. Learn to like it.

78

Anyone can come up with a reason why he or she hasn't succeeded (or can't succeed). Not surprisingly, those who don't succeed rarely blame themselves. That's hogwash. Lack of success begins first with those who fail for reasons wholly within their own control, not because of others or anything outside their control.

79

If something comes too easily, you haven't tried hard enough. Luck has nothing to do with it. As Thomas Edison said, "Genius is 1 percent inspiration, 99 percent perspiration." Don't accept what comes easily as all you need to do.

80

It's OK to be an American and proud of it. But it's not OK to be an ugly American.

81

Never regard your freedom as a privilege because you were lucky enough to be born here. Freedom is a right—a right for everyone. Pure and simple.

82

Miracles happen. Don't be suspicious when you are lucky enough to experience one.

83

The test of a relationship is not how easy it is to fall in love. The test is how difficult it is to fall out of love.

84

While there are always two sides to a story, it's rare for everyone to remember the facts as they truly were. Be careful when you take a side.

85

Unless restaurant service is really, really, really bad, tip 20 percent. Even servers have bad days. Never tip less than 10 percent.

86

If you're convinced a position you've taken is wrong, change your position. But only when you're convinced. Not when you're merely suspicious.

87

Don't worry about things you don't understand, like how a radio turns invisible signals in the sky into music. Some things just can't be explained.

88

When piglets grow up, they're still pigs. Unlike pigs, when adolescent boys grow up, they become men. Problem is, most adolescent boys never grow up.

89

There are some things you need to memorize. Your Social Security number. Your license-plate number. Your calling-card number. And your father's birthday.

90

If people lie to you, don't condemn them. No one can claim to have never lied. Make your judgments about people based on why they lied, not on the fact that they lied.

91

It's better to wear dirty underwear than no underwear at all.

92

If you ever wake up and you can't remember what you did the night before, you've got a serious problem. Don't blow it off as just another night out.

93

Colds come and go. They never win in the end. So don't let them slow you down. Ignore them.

94

You'll eventually get lines on your face whether you smile or frown. Might as well smile.

95

No one should address someone your parents' age by his or her first name unless the word "uncle" or "aunt" precedes it.

96

Drugs are meant to help with pain, disease, clinical depression, hair loss, and things the majority of people your age don't suffer from. They're not for recreation. You already know that. But I had to say it.

97

Being angry isn't a bad thing. Staying angry is.

98

They say elephants never forget. That's fine if you hang out with elephants. Otherwise, not only is forgetting normal, it's a really good thing.

99

Even when laughter hurts, it's good.

100

If there were one word I had to choose as the most powerful word I know, it would be "daddy." Not "dad." Not "father." "Daddy." It grabs my attention more than any word in the world.

101

No matter what you do, say, feel, become, or believe, I will always love you. Never doubt that.

Love,

Daddy
September 2002

To My Son, Joshua,
on Graduating College

1

In life, find the time to celebrate your successes. Graduating college is one such success. Enjoy that success with pride and celebration, and embrace the dawn of a wonderful adventure.

2

You've graduated from college. You never graduate from your family.

3

Relax and take a deep breath. You've earned it. And remember that there's no need to rush to your next place, wherever that may be.

4

You've had your share of mistakes. But take them in measure, and be reassured that while you'll err again as you move forward, no error can erase the many things you've accomplished and will achieve in the future. Overcome your mistakes; don't let them overcome you.

5

You may often be tempted to believe that the grass is greener somewhere else. On occasion, that may well be true. Just watch out for the weeds.

6

Don't misjudge greed for ambition. The former will lead you to failure, while the latter will bring you success. Know the distinction.

7

You once asked me not to tell you when I thought something you wanted to do was crazy. I told you that I'd never tell you anything you want to do is crazy, just perhaps a bit challenging. I meant it. The only thing that would be crazy is if you didn't challenge yourself. Now is the time to risk it. Risk losing it. And then risk it again.

8

Remember that home is where you can always heal your heart. You'll always have a key, a bed, and a person who will listen.

9

Don't worry about "finding yourself." Either you already have (and don't know it), or you'll find yourself in due time. I know you'll like the person you find.

10

It's possible that your first career after college will not be your last. But if you ever have to let it go, make sure you've learned what you can and you gave it your best shot.

11

Always give yourself options. Choose them carefully. There's no assurance they'll pay off. But having options affords you greater opportunity.

12

You will never stop being my son. You should never hesitate to ask me for a favor or for advice. Anything you might need is something I'd like to deliver. Whether I can or cannot deliver is the only issue, not my desire to do so.

13

You know the old line: "Sure you are a lot smarter now, but you still have a lot to learn." The line may be old, but it's nonetheless wise. Let others help you. Be humble but confident.

14

Every failure is a lesson, no matter how much that lesson may hurt. But remember, you are young and can afford to be hurt.

15

You've been given a lot of knowledge and made a lot of friends in your four years of college. Now begin to think how to give some knowledge and friendship back.

16

Don't mistake being scared for being challenged. There's very little to be afraid of and many challenges to embrace. When in doubt, give it a hug.

17

You've earned some time off. Take it.

18

Change is not a bad thing, no matter how much it may injure your ego. That's not to say you shouldn't be angry and hurt when forced to change, but the adage is absolutely true that time heals all wounds. The healing may be slow, but you will heal.

19

There's nothing more enlightening than to see in tough times how fast people jump ship, people who you would have thought would stand with you. So when someone does stand by your side in difficult times, that person is someone whose friendship you should cherish.

20

Until you're told you can't, you can. And when you're told you can't, don't believe it.

21

While it's not always easy to defend a difficult position or advance a worthy cause, you have an obligation to do so.

22

Learn to understand that being abandoned by others is not a reflection on you. It's a reflection on them. That's why they are led and do not lead.

23

Watch closely how people whom you know treat others. Make no mistake. When it suits their self-interest, they will treat you the same way. Don't be surprised.

24

Do not demand loyalty from those you protect, nurture, or mentor. You should protect, nurture, and mentor without any expectation of return.

25

Never lose faith in yourself, even when you fail. Remember that something got you to your position of leadership. When you fail (and you will on occasion), fall back on those strengths and rebuild from there.

26

Learn to let go of material things, remembering that they're just not important.

27

Forgiving is for priests and nuns. You don't need to always find a way to forgive. But do learn to forget.

28

Never be rash. Quick emotional decisions are more likely to hurt you than help you. Be patient.

29

Don't help those who fail cover their mistakes by drawing attention to you. Help them, but don't let them hide.

30

Voice your views logically and calmly, avoiding as much emotion as you can muster. That will not be easy. And when the emotion comes through, don't lament too long over it. Move on.

31

The twenty-four-hour rule makes sense. Let any decision you feel you must make sit for twenty-four hours. But in the end, regardless of the rule, make a decision.

32

One of the most difficult things in life is to figure out how to let go of anger. And the need to do it quickly. Anger only serves to narrow your opportunities and destroy your soul.

33

Friends may become distant in miles. But never let them become distant in your heart.

34

While there have been times I thought you might have done better or tried harder, remember that you've never disappointed me as my son, as a person, or as a spirit.

35

Your mother and I gave you your first breath, something we'll forever cherish. So if you ever lack faith in yourself and get a bit short of breath, you're one call away from some fresh air. Call us.

36

Some decisions you make in your life may hurt others. And while that's unavoidable, there's one decision that hurts the fewest—the right decision. Knowing the difference between the right ones and the wrong ones is what separates builders from those who destroy. Be a builder.

37

Know the difference between bosses and mentors. Work for a mentor. Quit bosses.

38

While you're through with exams, you'll never stop being tested. The only difference is that the tests will now challenge not just your knowledge but also your creativity, commitment, and character. And you'll pass them all with flying colors. You scored straight As in those subjects long before you went to college.

39

Don't expect those whom you respect and who were your mentors to always come to your side. Sooner than later, your success is largely your responsibility alone.

40

I know there's not much you can learn from me about women. But there's one piece of advice you should write down, read, and memorize. Tell it to yourself every day, year in, year out. The advice? Women are very strange and unexplainable. But that's what makes them so fascinating and exciting. Let them be strange.

41

Music has always been an important part of your life. Whether it's listening to a CD or playing the piano, music has fed the creativity in your soul. Never let that go. Listen. Play. Every day.

42

No matter how smart you become in solving your problems or how much experience you may have in facing your challenges, chances are I've been there, done that. And my advice is always free. That's an offer you can't refuse.

43

Men do cry.

44

The Golden Rule has nothing to do with religion. It has everything to do with your very heart and soul. Try to live it. But don't be surprised when you stumble or disappointed too long when you do.

45

In my day, fast cars, wild parties, and easy women were things we lusted for. Thank God I never got any of them. Well, I guess there were a fast car and some pretty good parties. But whatever you lust for, be careful. And trust me, there's one on that list—fast cars, wild parties, and easy women—you don't want (at least not too often). Can you guess which one to avoid?

46

If you can't make it home when you need to talk, call. A listening ear can work on the telephone just as well.

47

People who are perfect aren't very interesting. People who are imperfect are. If you're ever given a choice, surround yourself with imperfect people. Trust me, you'll all identify better with one another. I sure do.

48

OK. Four years as a slob. Dirty room. Clothes with a life of their own. Funny, multi-legged creatures as roommates. No rules. Consider it a vacation now ended. Welcome to the real world. It's not a bad place to be.

49

If you should take a detour now and again with a fast car or easy woman, make sure it's only a lease. Short term.

50

If you ever need my advice, all you have to do is ask. But remember, it's only advice. You don't have to agree. You don't have to follow it. You only need listen. And if you listen but decide not to follow my advice, please know that will never mean I won't give you advice again should you ask.

51

While your friends are very important in your life, your family is where you will always be anchored, and you should never let them be far from your mind, your heart, or your voice.

52

Back to wine and women. Finding the woman you want to spend the rest of your life with is like buying a fine wine. She will be older than you think and cost more money than you have. But she will taste better than anything you've ever drunk. Savor her vintage.

53

Being in the real world only means you have to dress a little better, make the dry cleaners your friend, accept that the floor is not a closet or dresser, and realize that bugs are indicative of a problem more acute than a couple of crumbs in a room. Obeying a few simple rules is no big deal; it's a cinch. In fact, the real world is a lot easier and more exciting than you might think.

54

Speaking of her, don't rush too fast finding her. You'll find each other in due time.

55

If you ever find the time to do all the things you want to do, that will mean you've run out of ideas, challenges, and goals. Don't go there.

56

You cannot appreciate what a wonderful country we live in and the freedom and opportunity it affords unless you see the world we live in. Travel. Better yet, travel without an itinerary.

57

Men don't ask for directions not because they won't admit they're lost but because they're proud that they're lost. Unless we're occasionally lost, we don't appreciate the effort of getting where we want to be.

58

Wine and women. Handle either one the wrong way, no matter how priceless they may be, and they'll turn to vinegar. And unless you're really into salads, you don't want to date, let alone marry, vinegar.

59

Your first career may not be the perfect career. Your second career might not be, either. In fact, the perfect career may never come. But never stop looking for it. Just make sure you don't mistake what you have as less than perfect too soon.

60

Boys' nights out are OK. Just don't make too much of a habit out of them.

61

If boys' nights out are OK, so are girls' nights out. You can't ask for room unless you give it to her as well.

62

Television is a great way to be distracted and entertained. But it's a terrible way to learn about what happened in the world on any given day. Read the paper. Read the newsweeklies. But read the comics, too.

63

They say that sons don't call their parents like daughters do. How about being an exception to the rule? We'll even accept the charges. Any time. Any day.

64

Most gas stations offer three grades of gas. One for the expensive cars, one for standard, reliable sedans, and one for the cars that run on cheap fuel. You can tell the difference just by listening to the engines. God made three kinds of women, too. And while it's great to have the expensive ones if you can afford them, it's never bad to have the reliable ones, either. Just don't drive with the ones who run on cheap fuel.

65

I do crosswords because they exercise my mind and challenge my vocabulary. And I don't even work up a sweat. Try it sometime. They're not just for old people.

66

When Mark Twain reached twenty-two, he was quoted as saying he was amazed at how much smarter his father had become since he was eighteen. I'm not sure if that's true or not for me, but I do know that I am truly amazed at how much smarter you've become since you were eighteen. It really doesn't matter how smart I am.

67

The difference between right and wrong is a bright line. Don't fool yourself and do the wrong thing because you think the difference is gray.

68

Whether you believe or not, give thanks to God every day. It's a nice way of saying how you appreciate all you've been given by whoever gave it to you.

69

It's easy for people to feel sorry for themselves. That takes no effort at all. And there are a lot of people who take that easy route. But the amazing ones are those who never feel sorry for themselves and always try to look on the brighter side of life. And you know what? They've got all the same problems as those who feel sorry for themselves. It's all simply a matter of perspective. Keep your perspective.

70

Let's find time to go to an occasional baseball game together.

71

Don't think you won't do wrong things. You have and you will again, as I have and will again. What's important is that you know you're fallible and that you not fall prey to thinking you need to be perfect. You don't. You need only be comfortable with yourself. That's a lot easier than you might think.

72

In case you haven't noticed, I've never stopped wanting to be your coach, even when I'm only a spectator. So when you need coaching, all you have to do is look to the bench. I'll be there—literally and spiritually.

73

If you only have the time to call either Mom or me, call Mom. I'll live with e-mail if you're too busy to call.

74

What some berate as daydreaming, I celebrate as reflection. Life is too short not to reflect a bit every day. So go ahead and waste some time daydreaming and reflecting.

75

Never having the time to do all the things you want to do is a wonderful thing. A nice place to be.

76

Writing is cathartic. Every time we write something down, we're revealing a little bit about our feelings, our beliefs, and ourselves. So jot down a few of your thoughts now and then. And if you're willing, I'd be honored to read them.

77

Don't prejudge who will be your allies if you need any. Many of those who do come to your side and support your views will surprise you. You may have to change your judgment dramatically on those you would least expect to take a stand with you.

78

Manage your anger; don't let it manage you. Always remember that anger eats a little of your soul each time you let it take control. You're better than that. Find a way to release your anger through talking, thinking, and forgetting. On the rare occasion when anger is a justified response, be sure to direct it at the cause of the anger, not just the person who might make you angry. Quite often the cause is more with you than with the actions of others.

79

Distinguish the difference between being alone and being lonely. There's nothing wrong with being alone. In fact, it's important to occasionally find the time to be alone, away from everyone. On the other hand, you need never be lonely. Friends are a call away. And so are your aunts and uncles. And so are your sisters. And so is your mother. And so is the rest of your family. Oh, and so am I. So how can anyone be lonely with a list that long?

80

People will disappoint you. As one person I know put it, most people are just ordinary. Their first priority is self-interest. But don't condemn even the ordinary. Just remember that you are extraordinary and someone who thinks first of others, then yourself. That's a lot easier than you think.

81

There is only one person you can be sure you'll be living with for the rest of your life—yourself. So take the time to become your own best friend.

82

Getting drunk is neither smart nor cool. It's just plain stupid. Take it from someone who knows. And take a lesson from yourself as well: remember each time you take a drink how easy it will be to get really stupid. Trust me; sobriety is a lot better than slobbery.

83

In a complex world, it's sometimes better to think of things in the simplest of forms—black or white, right or wrong, good or bad—and only then make your choice if you have a choice to make.

84

While there's nothing wrong with accepting things you cannot change, all too often, fear of failing to change something you believe is wrong is used to justify accepting what can be changed. It's better to fail than accept.

85

Remember your faith. Even go so far as to consider an occasional visit to church to reaffirm it. And if you're ever looking for a companion to go with you, I'd be happy to sing by your side, off-key and all.

86

Compromise your positions but never your principles.

87

There is such a thing as being a gentleman. Gentlemen open doors for women, help them on with their coats, let them go into (and out of) elevators first, make sure they don't have to slide across a seat when getting into a taxi, and much more. Trust me, being a gentleman pays off. Just like I told you playing the piano does.

88

There will be bad days. But no matter how bad they may be, they're better than the days of suffering and challenge borne by those steeped in poverty, war, and hatred. So keep even the worst of your days in perspective.

89

While negotiation is a fine art and one that you should strive to master, remember that you cannot negotiate with evil. You cannot negotiate with addiction. If you negotiate or rationalize with either one, you will lose. So no matter how skilled you may become in negotiating, don't fool yourself with the two opponents that never compromise.

90

I'm never too busy to get a call from you. Any time of the day, any day of the week. And if I'm not on the other end of the line when you call, I'll get back to you as soon as I can. But just in case I don't get right back to you, don't be afraid to call again. And again. And again.

91

Quite often, understanding why you do something you're not proud of is a futile exercise. Perhaps you'll never understand why. Rather than suffer the debate about why, try changing your patterns. Change the time you do things. Change the way you go places. Call people you haven't talked to in a while. Do something you've not done in a long time. If you change your patterns, the problems, as well as the "why" of the problems, may just fade away.

92

Never become comfortable with quitting.

93

Unless you're a little nervous and fearful of what you're doing, what you're doing won't lead you much of anywhere.

94

You don't measure someone's life by their successes or their wealth. You measure it by how they deal with their failures and share their wealth.

95

People will try to diminish your dreams and distract your direction. Listen. But never let go of your dreams.

96

Every day, I am fearful that I will lose the love of those I care about and the business of those I serve. But loss will never happen. Why? Because I fear every day that it will.

97

While I admire your ever-present desire to win, you must remember that winning must always be tempered with losses. Learn to be patient with the losses and modest with the wins.

98

Make sure there's always a designated driver. In fact, I'd be more than pleased to learn it's you.

99

Don't fall prey to your fears if confronted with a chance to explore, travel, or discover something new.

100

Break the stereotypes. Trust me, it won't hurt.

101

I witnessed a miracle the day you were born. And I've witnessed that miracle every day since as I've watched you grow and learn. And that's true no matter how far away you are. You make every day a miracle for me. Please never forget that. I love you, Josh. Carpe diem.

Love,

Dad
May 2004

To My Daughter, Andrea, on Beginning Her Career

What follows are some words of wisdom as you begin the next step in your journey through life. Much of what I write will seem obvious at first. That's OK. But many of the important things we forget are right in front of us—obvious yet missed. So—before you skim over one of my thoughts with the observation "Come on, Dad, I know that!"—give it a few moments of thought, and apply it to what you've experienced in life. Maybe you'll have one of those, "Wow, I forgot all about that one!" moments.

So sit back, relax, and consider this…

1

We learn from our mistakes more than we do from our successes. Sounds obvious enough, but how often do we dismiss our mistakes as soon as we can—and usually with a lame excuse? And how often do we relive our successes, almost to the point of excess? So maybe we should think a bit more about our failures and ask ourselves what we've learned and how we might avoid that mistake again. At the end of the day, measure your success by what you learn from the failures, and focus on the future.

2

Overachievers like you often see things from a negative perspective. It's what drives you. The trick is to find a balance between the negative and the positive. You need to learn to relish success and keep failure in perspective (but still learn from it). As you grow, you'll have your share of failures. We all do. But true success is achieved by adjusting to those failures and moving on to your next success.

3

Always try to be on time, but remember that it's better to be late to an appointment than early to your funeral. Now that's a pithy one, huh? But think about it: people who rush are careless, thoughtless, and rude. That's not you. Slow down and enjoy the ride, even if it's in bumper-to-bumper traffic.

4

Being optimistic is far harder than being pessimistic. Once you let yourself fall prey to the downward spiral of pessimism, inertia makes it harder and harder to hit reverse. So, no matter how bad it may seem, resist the downward spiral. And if you do find yourself in its grasp, fight like hell to pull out of it, and never, never, never give up.

5

Are you getting the message of optimism versus pessimism?
If not, go back to number 1.

6

When you encounter something odd, uncomfortable, or disconcerting, try this little exercise: raise your arms in the air and say aloud, "Fascinating." Really. Try it. I bet that thing that seemed so odd, uncomfortable, or disconcerting will seem pretty silly and insignificant.

7

I told your sister to remember that boys are pigs. I've reconsidered. And I've confirmed that boys *are* pigs. Yep. No doubt about it. Remember that.

8

Take care whom you invite into your life. Those who look good on the outside may be the devil on the inside. And once the devil is invited in, he doesn't leave easily. The corollary is equally true. Let the good people in. Because when you fail to invite the good people in because you judged them only by their surface, chances are they won't accept a second invitation.

9

That others you meet along life's road may be hurtful should come as no surprise. But whenever you're the hurtful person on your journey, you're on a detour to your demise. Stay on the good road and never be hurtful.

10

Whenever you leave an elevator, wish those who remain on the elevator a good day. It's a simple act of kindness that will surprise some people in a pleasant way, and it may just make their day.

11

Whenever you run into a cop or a fireman, thank him or her for what he or she does. Most people don't do that, and it does mean a lot. And he or she has earned the thanks.

12

There is an old Chinese saying: "A single act of carelessness leads to the eternal loss of beauty." Think about what that means. And avoid being careless in everything you do and say.

13

Call home when you can. The operative word is "call." Not e-mail. Not text. Call. We'd like to hear your voice on something more than your voice mail.

14

Never, never, never think you're safe in New York City. Or Boston. Or any city. Be aware.

15

A little glory for many is better than a lot of glory for a few. That's what teamwork is all about. (And it's a lot easier to succeed as a team than as an individual.)

16

When you delegate, you elevate. Don't hold on to everything just because you can do it. Delegate tasks to others. You free yourself up to do something else and do it better.

17

The corollary to 16, when you first begin your career, however, is not necessarily true. Don't let others delegate too much to you. Make sure you can deal with what you're assigned. Don't take on more than you can handle. Speak up.

18

When others to whom you've delegated fail, do not condemn them. Learn their limitations, and delegate to them again.

19

There is some truth in the thought "If you're afraid to take risks, go teach." That does not mean I don't respect teachers. I do. But they are not, by necessity, risk takers. Nor should they be. They're entrusted with building minds, and that is not a trust that should be risked. On the other hand, if you do decide to teach, remember the motto of the old Newark State College (now Kean University) scribed by John Cotton Dana: "Who Dares to Teach Must Never Cease to Learn."

20

Don't babysit partners and colleagues who can do things better than you. Let them run free.

21

A thought when you're an employee:
Let it go or be let go.

22

If you start high, you'll go higher. If you start low, you'll rise slower.

23

The easy things are for the idle. Push yourself.

24

Want to succeed in business? Remember FILO: first in, last out. That's the rule when you first start your career. As you grow, the only change is when you get in. Always be the last out.

25

FILO: first in, last out. That's a great philosophy in business, particularly when you begin your career. But be more cautious beyond your job. Taking risks is important, but knowing the difference between jumping in first and getting out last is not the way to approach risk. Be sensible.

26

Watch what you post. When in doubt, don't. Better yet, just don't.

27

You're human. You'll make mistakes. You'll miss obvious things. You'll occasionally hurt someone. It's OK. Just say you're sorry. And if your apology isn't accepted, don't expect much more from that person. If they don't accept your apology, they'll never accept you.

28

There is a very fine line between love and jealousy. Mistaking them is a common road we travel. Knowing the difference is the road to happiness.

29

When you first meet someone, learn about him or her before you talk about yourself. Ask where he or she is from, what he or she does, or what brings him or her to the place where you've met. Show humility and genuine interest in the person, and don't be concerned about what he or she thinks or knows about you. Take a deep interest in others, and they'll take a deeper interest in you.

30

Appreciate the economics and financial pressures others live with every day. Whatever your financial challenges may be, appreciating what plagues others keeps life in perspective.

31

Every once in a while, tell people you love how proud or impressed you are with what they've accomplished—personally and professionally.

32

Throw yourself a surprise party every once in a while.

33

Better yet, every once in a while, throw a surprise party for someone you love. But keep it a surprise. And remember, it doesn't have to be for a birthday. It's OK to throw one for any reason or for no reason at all. That's what makes them so surprising!

34

In relationships, the little things are important. Don't forget that. But lay off scolding someone like a child when he or she forgets. Instead, make a joke of it. Humor may not change a person as fast as ridicule, but it will ensure that person stays in your life a lot longer.

35

Try to understand a person's need to relax, and don't hit him or her with demands as soon as you see him or her. Make lists of what you need done or things you'd like to do.

36

Now and then, just say yes when someone suggests doing something rather than finding a reason not to—even when you think the suggestion is silly or when you think you have a better idea.

37

There is no challenge you can't meet, no problem you can't solve. There are only challenges and problems you fear taking on.

38

When you pass beggars in the street, give them some loose change. Sometimes, maybe even a dollar bill. It's OK to give a beggar a buck. You never know if he or she really needs it. And it's only a buck.

39

As a wonderful client of mine used to say, "Judge a person by the footprints they leave, not by the promises they make." What others have done cannot be erased, and it reflects who they are. What they promise can be easily forgotten. But remember their promises, too. Because those that are not fulfilled are as much a footprint as anything they've delivered.

40

I'm sometimes driven to poetry even though I'm a terrible poet. But when I'm struck to write a poem, it reflects a part of my soul. Try it, even if the poem is terrible (like mine). Here's one I wrote when I was thinking about you, Meg, Josh, and Mom:

With the dawn of each day, my thoughts of family cleanse my soul
I become free of fear, full of hope, and gratefully faithful
Thankful that God gave me the gift to share my life with others
As His miracle reminds me that to them I owe my life.

41

Let your spirit soar to heights as high as your dreams, but keep your nightmares only as memories of fantasies forgotten.

42

The touch of a person's love is a deeply taken elixir—like a cup running over with vintage wine. Drink it up.

43

Remember that whatever occurs in the world or whatever happens in your life, no matter how personally upsetting it may be, it's going to be OK. The bad things will pass with time. You'll always heal. Together we can all heal one another if we let ourselves. And if we don't heal for some reason, that's God's way, and that's OK, too.

44

You have choices. You can be an individual who, when knocked down, gets up, dusts off, and looks to a wonderful day ahead. Or you can choose to never see beyond your personal challenges, accepting them in defeat. Personally, I don't think you're accepting of defeat.

45

Here's a toast to tomorrow. Another bright day to live to its fullest.

46

Don't trust the news reported on television and in most newspapers. In their search for subscribers and ratings, the truth is lost. And don't trust politicians. Any of them. They're worse than the news.

47

Every day is a celebration of living, knowing that there will always be heroes in times of strife, saviors in time of pain, and friends in times of need—friends who might not have been friends just seconds before but who become lifelong friends in the flash of an instant. So remember that when you face strife, pain, and need, someone will help.

48

While there's a lot you'll never understand and too much you'll be asked to forgive, you must not lose sight of the fact that you show your true humanity when your back is to the wall and when you're treated with less respect than you're due. That's when you must put behind you petty prejudices, anger, hatred, and bigotry. And while there will be much you must simply accept for what it is, never shy away from asking why. Getting answers is the only way you'll ever find truth.

49

The pop culture we live with today is a reflection of what we do to relax in a world that is all too easily overwhelming. There's no point in being generationally judgmental. We should be grateful for pop culture and its diversion.

50

Without question, life can be overwhelming at times. The trick to getting through the moments when they seem too much to bear is to talk. Keeping it inside yourself will only make the burden less bearable and, eventually, unbearable. Talk to someone you care about. Talk to someone who cares about you.

51

My parents were an inspiration, particularly my mom. Whenever I feel depressed or left out, I think of them. I think of how my father was a hero in war and my mom a beacon of hope in the worst of times. That all helps get through whatever challenges I face. It's what family is all about. Remember that.

52

In writing about my mom, a good friend observed, "If I could pass on to my children just a fraction of her magical positive attitude, her incredible strength of will, or her unfailing belief that everything ultimately works out for the best, I would consider that a wonderful legacy." So would I.

53

If I could remove just one word from my vocabulary, it would be "no." But "maybe" is OK.

54

Diversions are important. Diversions might be meditating, exercise, travel, music, theater, a good TV show, books, art, writing, and more. They're all good diversions. Don't let anyone tell you that you're wasting your time on them. The truth is that it's your time to waste, and only you can decide if you're doing so wisely.

55

When speaking, avoid speech disfluency. What, you might ask, is "speech disfluency?" According to dictionary. com, it's defined as "impairment of the ability to produce smooth, fluent speech" or "an interruption in the smooth flow of speech, as by a pause or the repetition of a word or syllable." So don't say, "Like, we were together for, like, an hour before he, like, said hello." Instead, say, "We were together for an hour before he said hello." The use of the word "like" makes speech prone to disfluency. Listen to yourself sometimes. Do you, like, get it? Rid your vocabulary of the word "like," and confine its use to Facebook.

56

Pets are fine. But normal pets. Not an iguana. Not a pig. Not a snake. A dog. Or a cat. And give them a decent name. What you name a pet reflects upon you. Give it a dumb name, and well, you're dumb, too.

57

The saying goes, "A mind is a terrible thing to waste." Worse, not having an open mind guarantees a wasted mind. Listen first; judge last.

58

Write. Write. Write. If you don't write down your goals, thoughts, and aspirations, you're less likely to achieve them.

59

Never stop traveling. Being home is nice, but not at the price of exploration and discovery. And when you meet someone who seems small-minded, ask him or her where he or she has traveled. I'll bet nowhere that would teach him or her humility or humanity.

60

A good night's sleep is important and helps make sure you have a good next day. But a bad night's sleep should never mean you'll have a bad next day. "I'm tired" is not an excuse. It's a cop-out.

61

We all have opinions. We all make judgments. But when our opinions and judgments turn into criticism and argument, our opinions are shallow and our judgment is flawed.

62

In traffic, if someone cuts in front of you, yield to them. Even if it keeps you from arriving on time. Not only will it be safer, but the other person may legitimately be in a hurry. Or may be stupid. Either way, yield.

63

Call me.

64

Call Mom.

65

If you have to choose whether you'll call Mom or me, call Mom.

66

Jobs are just layovers in your life's journey. Don't let them become a final stop too soon.

67

Give gifts. Just do it. Gifts are cool to give.

68

Gift getting: even better than gift giving. Sound selfish? It is. But it's honest. The saying that it is better to give than to receive is flat-out wrong. When it comes to getting gifts—bring 'em on!

69

Life throws us curves everyday—some good, some bad. So remember that each time you say good-bye to someone, it may be the last time—God forbid—you ever see that person again. So never forget to say good-bye, and always leave that person feeling you care about him or her and look forward to seeing him or her again. Even consider giving him or her a hug.

Words

So far, most of what I've had to say is pithy, sometimes humorous advice. And while I'm serious about what I've said and hope it's given you some reason to think about important things in your life, the next thirty-one are different. They're serious, albeit with a dose or two of humor. The next thirty-one are a dictionary of words—powerful words. Some are definitions and some have explanations, but all offer advice.

70

Moms. There is a bond between mother and child that is unlike any other. I'm not sure if that's because of the many months of pregnancy, the miracle of being the one who gave life to a child, or something else. It doesn't matter. So when a child is disappointed, feels forgotten, gets angry, or becomes stressed with his or her mom, that child must never forget and must always trust and appreciate the bond and the love of his or her mother. Nothing can break that bond.

71

Moms and daughters. The relationship between a mother and daughter is a mystery and marvel that sometimes confounds me. Mothers are very protective of their young. Get between a mother and her child, and you're asking for more trouble than you can imagine. Yet with daughters, moms sometimes seem a bit more critical. A bit more concerned. I've come to believe that's true because they know, unlike dads, the challenges women face and the sacrifices they're asked to make in life. They identify with their daughters. They want their daughters to learn to cope better and not fall into the hands of life's predators. Understand that, and you understand that the occasional criticism is well intentioned and justified.

72

Moms and sons. With sons, a mom's relationship is a bit different than it is with daughters. Moms are just as protective. They're just as concerned. But they also seem less stressed about how their sons will fare with life's challenges. That is not meant as a chauvinistic statement. It's just an observation. Have no doubt that if you cross a mother with regard to a son, you'll also face a wrath like you've never seen.

73

Dads. Most dads don't stay at home, so they don't get to see their children as much as they'd like. For some, the time they can spend with their children only lessens as years pass. That makes the moments together all the more important for both the dad and the child. The reality is that it's a tough balance. But for the good dads, it's well worth the effort.

74

Dads and daughters. What can I say? Maybe it's genetic, maybe not. But for the most part, dads don't know how to say no to daughters, even when they should. I remember one time when I was driving Josh and Meghan somewhere. Josh was in the front seat and Meghan in the back. It was quiet. No one was talking. Then from the backseat came one word in the form of a question: "Daddy?" Josh looked at me and said, "You're dead." Clearly, "Daddy" coming from a daughter is the most powerful word in the world. And an unfair advantage!

75

Dads and sons. I bet Josh only wishes that "Dad" from a son were as powerful as "Daddy" from a daughter. Not. I guess dads just naturally push their sons and often expect more from them. That's entirely unfair, but it's reality. Why should that matter to you? After all, you're a daughter with a clear advantage with me. It should matter to you because some day you'll marry someone's son. And when you do, note what I said about moms and sons and dads and sons. It may help you understand a lot about your husband.

76

Parents, part one. Mom and I will never stop acting like parents, whether you're under our roof or not. So when we act concerned, we are simply being parents. When we give you advice, we do so because we've "been there, done that," as all parents have. And when we ask you not to do something, we ask you not because we don't trust you but because we understand the world a bit better than you—just like other parents. Parenting is a job you never quit and one that never ends. But it's also the most rewarding job anyone can ever hope to have. If you're ever blessed with children, you'll understand that some day. But until then, try and understand.

77

Parents, part two. Parents are confusing. They're compassionate yet demanding. They push you to achieve. They often have no patience and little tolerance or understanding of excuses. They insist that you never look down on anyone. They teach you to respect God. They let you grow but not too fast. They give you laughs. They let you cry. They make you angry. And they leave you full of memories. But above all else, they love you.

78

Brothers and sisters. Siblings can seem like competitors or even, occasionally, enemies. However unsettling that may sometimes be, it's really quite normal. But siblings who let competition or anger overshadow the love sisters and brothers have for one another will lose more than friends; they'll lose their hearts. Brothers and sisters can decide not to forgive friends and colleagues. But they must always forgive their sisters and brothers. Sisters and brothers reflect their moms, dads, and family. Whatever relationships you may lose in life, whether or not by choice, you must never risk losing relationships within your family. Even if that means occasionally eating crow.

79

Children. There is nothing—absolutely nothing—more rewarding for me than being your father. That goes for Josh and Meghan, too. Having the three of you made me better understand miracles and the wonders God creates. It has taught me more about love and responsibility than I could have ever learned without the three of you. And it's given me more pride than I can ever measure. Anyone who has not seen the miracle of birth and experienced all that a child brings to one's life will never understand what being a parent is all about.

80

Family. Jealousy, anger, greed, and just about every negative attribute a person can have are found in every family. But that does not detract from the singular importance of family—relationships that are born from generations of common connections. Those connections become most important when times are at their toughest. So no matter how disappointing a family member may become, remember that he or she is family. And family comes first.

81

Death. Nasty. Inevitable. We all have to deal with it eventually—both for ourselves and our loved ones. But it's not something that should occupy our minds for more than an instant except when it is imminent. That just invites pain and paralysis. It does you no good. And when death does steal someone from you, grieve. That's healthy. But also remember all the wonderful things that person gave to you and others, and try to live with him or her in mind, knowing he or she is watching. Make him or her proud.

82

Marriage. Marriage can be hard, but it should be. Great things do not come or grow easily. So if you should ever marry, remember that marriage is the one highway in life where the driving is shared, detours are best avoided, and exits are closed.

83

Divorce. No. Yes. It depends. Divorce is too easy an out. A failure for at least one of the partners. And a sad loss for both. And more often than not, worse for children. It should always be an absolute last resort. Marriage can be a fight, but divorce is a knockout.

84

Love. Understanding love is best expressed by word association: wonder, beauty, passion, caring, mystery, confusion, pain, heartache, elation, pride, jealousy, admiration, loss, success, failure, distance, closeness, sustenance, sharing, honesty, lies, selfishness, sacrifice, support, and safety. It's a roller coaster. But it's also the ride of your life, and the more times you get the privilege to ride that roller coaster, the better your life will be. Don't be afraid to love someone or to be loved.

85

Abortion. For me, a woman's choice. That doesn't mean, however, that everyone will accept it or understand it. But no one should preach condemnation for it. If condemnation is deserved, that's up to God, not churches, politicians, or religious zealots.

86

Lifestyle. A personal choice. But that doesn't mean everyone will be comfortable around alternative lifestyles. That discomfort is not necessarily a rejection. Most likely, it's caused by prejudice or ignorance, but on occasion, it might simply be something a person feels and, perhaps, believes. Even for some with an open heart. So while it's OK to try to help someone overcome prejudice or ignorance, know the difference between that and true beliefs (however much you may disagree with him or her). Don't force a false comfort just so that you can feel better. And be careful when you choose to condemn someone for his or her beliefs. At times, he or she deserves condemnation. But sometimes he or she doesn't.

87

Sacrifice. Sacrifice can hurt. It's a true measure of a person's compassion, particularly when one sacrifices for someone he or she doesn't even know or for an ideal that's worth protecting. In your life, you'll be asked to make sacrifices. When you are, think about the needs of those who ask or the importance of the ideals the sacrifice supports. And when you see or read about others who sacrifice, particularly those who risk or give their lives so we can safely live ours, be thankful.

88

America. America is hard to understand. Yet it's the most respected nation in the world. It stands for principles unlike any other country in history. While it certainly has flaws and is all too often led by frauds, there is no better place to live and work. If you doubt that, travel. Try to learn about America. Read the Declaration of Independence and the Constitution. I can hear you now: "Oh, come on, Dad, why do I need to read them?" Don't dismiss that suggestion so quickly. I know you'd like to. That's a mistake. So do me a favor: read those two documents. I've read them many times. I even have them on my iPhone.

Yeah, there's an app for that. So please read them. I'd be happy to answer any questions you might have!

89

Voting. It's your right to vote. It's also your right not to vote. I respect that as a principle. And when you do vote, I don't care whom you vote for. That's your decision. But not voting is tantamount to saying that you don't care or have given up. If that's true, fine. But don't complain about government, taxes, regulation, or politics. When you vote, you participate and earn the right to an opinion that should be listened to. Opinions of those who don't vote don't sway me, and frankly, I don't want to even hear them.

90

Bullying versus passion. Know the difference between bullying and passion. Never bully. But never lose your passion. And when someone accuses you of being a bully when you're being passionate, don't let up. He or she is the one being a bully.

91

Bigotry versus prejudice. There is never a justification for bigotry, but sometimes there is for prejudice. There are people who are evil, dangerous, and undeserving of respect. Many of them can never be changed. And they come in all races, creeds, and religions. They spew idiotic ideals and ideas. As long as your prejudice is against those individuals, prejudice is fine. But when your prejudice is based on race, creed, religion, or the right to have ideas or ideals you don't personally approve of, then that's bigotry. And there is never room for bigotry.

92

Competition. Competition is not about winning. Sure, winning is important, but a win not honestly achieved is not a victory. It's a failure. True competition is about being fair and honest, trying your best to achieve goals, and succeeding through effort, not deceit. That doesn't mean others won't cheat to win, but don't fall into that hole. If you do, you'll never get out, and you'll eventually lose.

93

Leadership. Leadership is rarely something that gets a thank-you, so don't expect it. But don't shy from being a leader or be upset when you don't get recognition. Remember that being a leader sure beats the view from behind.

94

Past versus future. Speculative predictions of the future will never match the lessons of the past.

95

Holidays versus every day. Celebrating once-a-year things like holidays, birthdays, and anniversaries is a good thing. But celebrating life and God's gifts to us every day is a great thing.

96

Heartbreak. I suppose you can truly break someone's heart, but we all too often let disappointments or letdowns become heartbreaks in our minds. They're not. You survive. You get over disappointment and letdowns. You even get over heartbreak.

97

Charity. Being generous and charitable is important. But remember two things about charity: first, not everyone who asks for it deserves it. Be careful to whom you decide to be charitable. Check him or her out. Regrettably, there are simply too many scams. Second, true charity is often given anonymously. If you find yourself giving because you want recognition or respect, don't get too carried away with your generosity. You sold it for a price.

98

Honesty. You know the saying that "it always pays to be honest." And for the most part, that's true. But as true as it may be, there are definitely times when honesty is a really bad idea. You should always ask yourself if being honest can be hurtful. So don't tell your loved ones that they dress poorly, need a haircut, or have stupid ideas. Keep that honesty to yourself. But when your loved ones need an honest moment to prevent them from hurting themselves or others, go for it. Just choose honesty that is helpful, not hurtful.

99

Miracles. I was privileged to watch the miracle of your birth. Anyone who does not believe birth is a miracle is a fool. We also witness miracles when a flower blooms, a rainbow appears, or a life forgotten is saved. And I witness a miracle every time I see you.

100

Religion. Religion is easy to criticize and even easier to ignore. It begs too many questions and provides too few answers. But without it, God is too easily forgotten. Religion is the vessel we need to remember God on what we hope is a trip to redemption. Which religion you practice doesn't matter. But adopt one or go to hell.

101

I love you. I am proud of you. That will never change.

Love,

Daddy
August 2013

About the Author

Doulgas J. Wood practices law in New York City and is the author of *Presidential Intentions*, a novel of political fiction and the first woman to run for president of the United States, and *Please Be Advised: A Legal Reference Guide for the Advertising Executive.*

About the Cover

Robert Frost wrote a wonderful poem entitled A Road Not Taken. Its closing verse reads, "Two roads diverged in a wood, and I – I took the one less traveled by, And that has made all the difference." The cover illustrates a road less traveled. One I hope my children find, take and discover all the wonderful things life's journey has to offer them.

Proof

Made in the USA
Charleston, SC
04 June 2014